My
Unflappable
Mum

My Unflappable Mum

An Appreciation *of* Mothers

Images by Jonathan Chester

Words by Patrick Regan

Andrews McMeel Publishing, LLC

Kansas City · Sydney · London

Andrews McMeel Publishing, LLC
an Andrews McMeel Universal company
1130 Walnut Street, Kansas City, Missouri 64106

www.andrewsmcmeel.com

13 14 15 16 17 SDB 10 9 8 7 6 5 4 3 2 1

ISBN: 978-1-4494-3564-6

ATTENTION: SCHOOLS AND BUSINESSES
Andrews McMeel books are available at quantity
discounts with bulk purchase for educational, business,
or sales promotional use. For information, please
e-mail the Andrews McMeel Publishing Special Sales
Department: specialsales@amuniversal.com

Introduction

*"Making the decision to have a child—it's momentous.
It is to decide forever to have your heart go walking around
outside your body."* —Elizabeth Stone

It's the world's hardest job, with the worst pay, and benefits that won't show up on any spreadsheet. It's twenty-four hours a day, every day, and each rising sun brings a new set of hurdles and hassles that only get replaced with tougher ones as the years go by.

It's motherhood, and it's no place for sissies.

Those with a basic knowledge of biology know that it's pretty simple to become a mother (though the final push is no picnic), but becoming a good mum is anything but easy. Becoming a great one is harder still. And becoming one of the best? Well, that's an honour reserved for a select few . . . like you, the amazing and exalted, the most rare of birds—the incredible, unflappable mum.

Mums are fluent in many languages.

The babblings of a baby, the ramblings of a toddler, the body language of adolescents, and the foreign tongue spoken by teenagers—the best mums can decipher them all.

Master the fine art of simply being there.

Words do not always need to be said. Grand gestures are rarely required. A parent who is present, emotionally and physically, is a gift. Period.

There's one on every block.

The fun mum. The expert blanket-fort builder. The lemonade-stand organizer. The mum all the neighbor kids love. The one who was never too busy to play—or at least made us feel that way. That's the mum I was lucky enough to have.

The Incredible Invisible Mum

To the casual observer, it might sometimes appear that mums are invisible to their offspring. For all the effect her words have, one might even assume that a mother speaks at a frequency inaudible to her children. Why is it that when you want their attention, you don't exist, but when you need a little quiet, they won't leave you alone?

Nobody's Fool

Every mum should wear a badge that reads, "Don't even try." Don't even try to lie about who tracked in the mud, who flattened the just-about-to-bloom daffodils with a football, or who started the fight that led to the three-day suspension. Veteran mums aren't just unflappable—they're unfoolable. As Spanky from *Our Gang* memorably said, "You can fool some of the people some of the time, but you can't fool Mom."

Accept all, find beauty in each.

Every kid is gifted—some physically, some intellectually, and some in ways not as quick to emerge or as easy to categorise. Wise mums know the fundamental truth—there's pure beauty at the heart of every child.

Take the long view.

From the adolescent point of view, every pimple is Vesuvius. Every setback is the own goal that loses the World Cup. Every rejection is a rejection from the universe itself. Mums know better. Experience equals perspective. Bad day today? Guess what? A new one starts tomorrow.

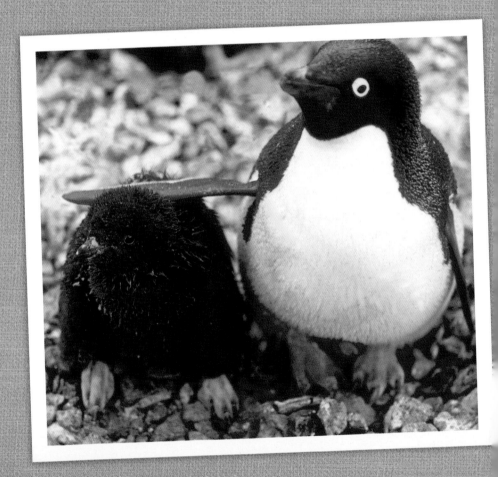

Under the wing is a tricky thing.

There's a fine line between gentle guidance and overbearing oppression. The best mums instinctively know when to shelter and when to back off.

"Mother" spoken here.

Conversations between mums often begin like this: "You'll never guess what that little (expletive) has done this time. . . ." Mums have a language all their own, rife with terms of endearment, terms of frustration, and—akin to that old (apocryphal) saying about Eskimos and snow—at least one hundred words for "tired." Luckily, mums have each other with whom to share woes, battle stories, secrets, and the little sustaining daily triumphs, too.

Rise above
the crap.

A mother's life is filled with it—
literally for the first few years and
figuratively thereafter. When it
comes to sheer volume and variety,
nobody is called upon to put up
with as many piddling annoyances
as Mum.

There's no snuggle like a mum snuggle.

Biologists posit that penguin parents and chicks identify each other by scent and unique vocalizations. Although no fieldwork has yet been conducted to support this related theory, we wouldn't be surprised if there's another way that chicks know their mums—the snuggle. Nothing else feels so warm, so right, so like love and home, as nestling into Mum.

She'd give the feathers off her back if she could.

Penguin mums (dads, too) feed their chicks right out of their mouths. While the corollary behaviour isn't as direct (or slimy), their human compatriots in parenting certainly know all about giving their young the food off their plate. "You'd like more potatoes? Here, Love, have mine." Call it the Mum Diet.

Call for time out.

Being a pal to your kid is fun.
It's easy. It's also a recipe for disaster.
No decent parent takes pleasure in
disciplining her kids, but then again,
no one said this was an easy gig.
A game of pillow kickball in the living
room? That was probably Dad's idea.
The concept of time out? Almost
certainly invented by a mum.

Memo from Mum: Get off your bum.

Life is not a video game. You don't get extra lives. Mums know that the "power-ups" that really count are fresh air, exercise, nutritious meals, and a healthy home atmosphere. "Turn it off. Get off the couch. Go outside and play." Those are sage words of wisdom from the original "life coach"—Mum.

This too shall pass.

Sulky one minute, manic the next. Teenagers really do seem like a different species altogether. So, what's a mum to do? Well, not a lot, actually. The best mums seem to know instinctively that adolescence is a part of life's journey that requires a fair amount of self-navigation. Young adults are contemplating a vast, blank landscape known as the rest of their lives. Let them explore. Let them try on different personalities and decide for themselves who they want to be.

At your own peril

We all know what a mother's love is, right? Unconditional. Nurturing. Warm and fuzzy. Know what else it is? Fierce. Agatha Christie once wrote, "A mother's love for her child is like nothing else in the world. It knows no law, no pity. It dares all things and crushes down remorselessly all that stands in its path." Bam. How's that for warm and fuzzy?

When life's not fair, she'll be there.

Kids can be cruel. Good guys don't always finish first. Dark clouds are not contractually obligated to have silver linings. No one likes to be the bearer of bad news or the deliverer of harsh realities—especially to wide-eyed kids who believe in goodness and magic. The sorting out of difficult truths is best done by empathetic professionals. That means mums. No one can match them when it comes to weaving the tough stuff in among the goodness and magic (and, yes, life holds plenty of that, too).

You are being watched.

Sure there are days (years, even) when mums would swear kids pay no attention to what they say or do. The truth is they are always observing— and subconsciously filing away what they see and hear.

Influences are everywhere. Decent role models are not. Let's face it, no "real housewives" of anywhere are going to teach kids the proper way to behave, to carry themselves, and to mature. Only real mums can do that.

One clear moment

Ask a hundred mothers what gift they'd most like to receive. A blue-boxed bauble from Tiffany? A kitchen remodel? A couch sans Magic Marker hieroglyphs? All would finish a distant second to that one thing most precious and elusive to mums— time. Time to reset. Time to reflect. Time to reacquaint with that person she used to know so well—herself.

A mum for all seasons

It's not hard to be happy in good times. And it's natural to be down in the bad. What really distinguishes a person is how she carries herself on a grey day— when the sun doesn't shine, no fresh breeze blows, and the world seems to wallow in blah. Who always manages to tease beams of brightness out of a grey day? Indispensible, incandescent, effervescent Mum.

Full immersion

A mother's love doesn't materialise out of the blue at the moment of delivery. It isn't born at that first instance of eye-to-eye, but long, long before. It begins as a love borne of possibility. Then anticipation. A mother's love grows as her baby grows inside, building in intensity, so when the babe finally does arrive, she finds herself positively immersed in the stuff. The transition (from shell to nest, from womb to cradling arms) isn't easy, but the saturation of a mother's love makes it the most natural thing in the world.

House Beautiful can wait

To be a mother is to master the art of prioritisation. For most mums, a typical day's to-do list goes something like this: Wake kids (or be awakened by small kids), feed kids, dress kids, drive kids, pick up after kids, worry about kids, drive kids some more, feed kids, clean kids, put kids to bed, crash . . . and repeat. So, yes, if the home front gets to looking a little rough by the end of the week, so be it. This is not a magazine shoot. This is real life.

Coping secrets of the successful mum

When behaviour is relentlessly bad, when patience wears thin and energy wears out, experienced mums know that there's a reward waiting at the end of the day. (And not just the one served in a tall-stemmed glass.) When the day is done, she can tiptoe into the bedroom and see her "little angels" quietly, blissfully sleeping. It's even better than wine for forgetting and forgiving the battles of the day.

Here's the thing about dirt . . . it washes away.

Cot is swapped for big-boy bed seemingly overnight. Toddling becomes tearing around the house in a flash. Nappies to Pull-Ups to big-girl panties. Pram to tricycle to scooter to bike. Childhood speeds. Adolescence is a blur. From a rearview perspective, the years we have with our children are fleeting and golden. Yes, they come home muddy once in a while. Someday—and it won't be long—they won't be coming home at all. Would any mother trade the mess for the memories?

47

Let them go.

It's a mum's job to be ever watchful, fiercely protective, and deeply engaged in her children's lives. It's also a mum's job to let go—to send them into the big scary world, whether that means walking away without looking back on the first day of nursery school or nudging them gently out of the nest as young adults. Self-reliance and a sense of adventure are two of the best gifts mums can give.

Always enough

Whether it's a houseful of her own kids or someone else's, and whether they deserve it or not, there is always enough love to go around. No matter how weary, how frazzled, how worried she may be, the reservoir of love that is Mother never gets depleted. How do mums do it?

There's everyone else, then there's Mum.

The whole world over, my whole life through, there'll never be anyone who means so much to me as my unmatchable, unforgettable, unflappable mum.

Image key

Front Cover
Chinstrap penguins
Pygoscelis antarctica
Though they can occur all around
Antarctica, chinstrap breeding
populations are concentrated on
the Antarctic Peninsula where
an estimated 99% of the world's
population occurs.

Page 7
Emperor penguins
Aptenodytes fosteri
Amery Ice Shelf
Emperor penguin chicks begin to
lose their downy feathers (fledging)
in November and December when
they are between 100 and 150
days old.

Page vi
Chinstrap penguins
Half Moon Island, South Shetland
Islands
Always clamoring to be fed,
chinstrap chicks grow rapidly on
a diet of regurgitated krill. They
get fed twice daily for the first two
weeks, then less regularly as they
get larger.

Page 8
Adélie penguins
Antarctic Peninsula
When it is warm, the well-insulated
Adélie penguins will hold their
flippers akimbo for maximum
cooling effect from the blood vessels
that are close to the skin in the less
densely feathered areas of their
bodies.

Page 3
Chinstrap penguins
Half Moon Island, South Shetland
Islands
Pairs of chicks are common, but if
the clutch is reduced to one chick,
the surviving bird grows much
faster.

Page 10
Chinstrap penguins
Half Moon Island, South Shetland
Islands
With global warming, the Antarctic
Peninsula is often above freezing
and the rookeries become mud
puddles when it rains, or the snow
melts.

Page 4
Adélie penguins
Pygoscelis adelie
Antarctic Peninsula
When there are few adults around
for protection, older Adélie chicks
gather together in clusters called
crèches.

Page 12
Chinstrap penguins
Half Moon Island, South Shetland
Islands
Chinstraps occupy the highest
rocky points suitable for nesting, as
these are the first to become snow
free and in turn offer the longest
potential breeding period.

Page 14
Adélie penguins
Cape Denison, Commonwealth Bay
Adélie chicks grow rapidly and within weeks they are too large to shelter under the parent in a rocky nest. Up until this point the parents take turns at guarding their offspring.

Page 22
Chinstrap penguins
Antarctic Peninsula
Regurgitated shrimplike crustacea, Antarctic krill, is fed to the chicks in multiple extended feeding sessions when the adult returns from foraging.

Page 16
Rockhopper penguins
Eudyptes chrysocome
New Island, Falkland Islands
Rockhopper penguin adults identify themselves to their mates minding the nest with a series of vocalizations each time one of them returns from feeding.

Page 25
Adélie penguins
Cape Denison, Commonwealth Bay
The dense down plumage Adélie chicks acquire by three weeks of age is just one of the many adaptations that enable them to survive in extreme conditions.

Page 19
Gentoo penguins
Pygoscelis papua
Brown Bluff, Antarctic Peninsula
Gentoos nest on rocky coastal beaches and the colonies become whitewashed with acrid-smelling guano. Its color is an indication of their diet. White suggests a diet predominantly of fish.

Page 27
King penguins
South Georgia
King penguin chicks grow to a very large size and look so different from their parents that at first early explorers thought they were a different species.

Page 21
Adélie penguins
Antarctic Peninsula
For the first three weeks after the chicks hatch, Adélie parents take daylong turns at minding their offspring.

Page 29
Emperor penguins
Amery Ice Shelf
Fledging emperor penguin chicks gain their juvenile plumage in November and December, by which time they are ready to go to sea to begin foraging for themselves.

55

Page 30
Gentoo penguins
Antarctic Peninsula
A gentoo breeding pair takes turns at incubating their eggs for an average of 35 days before hatching occurs.

Page 33 and Back Cover
King penguins
Apetendoytes patagonica
South Georgia
King penguins can raise only one chick at a time because a pair takes turns at balancing a single egg on their feet during the incubation phase. The resulting chick is reared over such an extended time that a pair can breed only twice every three years.

Page 34
Emperor penguins
Amery Ice Shelf
Emperor penguins are the largest and most majestic of all the penguin species. Adults measure between 44 and 52 inches in height (110 and 130 cm), and their fledglings are bigger than the adults of all other penguin species, barring the king penguin.

Page 37
Chinstrap penguins
Half Moon Island, South Shetland Islands
Penguins never really sleep soundly for fear of predation, but they often nap standing up for minutes at a time, any time of day or night.

Page 38
Adélie penguins
Antarctic Peninsula
Red guano covering the colony indicates the Adélies have been feeding predominantly on Antarctic krill.

Page 41
Gentoo penguins
Antarctic Peninsula
On the Antarctic Peninsula in December, breeding gentoos begin laying two similarly sized eggs within a three-day period.

Page 42
Gentoo penguins
Brown Bluff, Antarctic Peninsula
Gentoos make stone nests to help keep eggs and chicks above melt-water should the temperature rise sufficiently to produce rain or snow melt.

Page 44
Gentoo penguins
Antarctic Peninsula
For protection gentoo chicks gather in crèches at four to five weeks of age, allowing both parents to go to sea to feed.

Page 46
Adélie penguins
Antarctic Peninsula
Without a good waterproof coating
on their downy feathers, Adélie
penguin chicks are vulnerable to
rain and cold.

Page 53
Adélie penguins
Antarctic Peninsula
Adélie penguin adults and their
chicks have feathers to the very
tip of their bills, one of the many
adaptations giving them the ability
to survive the extreme conditions.

Page 48
Emperor penguins
Antarctic Peninsula
Emperor penguin chicks are often
small when they first have to go to
sea to fend for themselves. However,
this occurs at the beginning of
summer when the food supply is
plentiful, so they are able to survive.

Page 51
Emperor penguins
Amery Ice Shelf
In October and November, emperor
chicks move about in groups. They
huddle when the weather is bad,
waiting for their parents, both
of which go to sea to forage. As
summer approaches, the distance to
the feeding grounds decreases and
the parents can return daily or every
other day to feed their chick. Once
nearby, they identify each other with
a series of trilling calls.

About the Authors

Jonathan Chester is a veteran polar photographer. The photographs in this book are from his many Antarctic expeditions. Patrick Regan has written lots of books—some with penguins, some without. You can learn more about Jonathan and Patrick and their books at extremeimages.com and patrickreganbooks.com.

Chester and Regan previously collaborated on the books *Flipping Brilliant: A Penguin's Guide to a Happy Life, To Love Is to Fly,* and *Stay Cool: A Polar Bear's Guide to Life.*

This book is dedicated with great love and thanks to our own unflappable mums: Thyra Yvette Chester and Patty Regan.

—JC & PR